Charos Uralova

Sardor Tukhtayev

ARTICLE WRITING PROCEDURES

© Taemeer Publications LLC
Article Writing Procedures
by: Charos Uralova, Sardor Tukhtayev
Edition: February '2024
Publisher:
Taemeer Publications LLC (Michigan, USA / Hyderabad, India)

ISBN 978-93-5872-756-2

© **Taemeer Publications**

Book	:	Article Writing Procedures
Author	:	**Charos Uralova, Sardor Tukhtayev**
Publisher	:	Taemeer Publications
Year	:	'2024
Pages	:	74
Title Design	:	*Taemeer Web Design*

TABLE OF CONTENTS

INTRODUCTION 5

GENERAL INFORMATION ABOUT THE ARTICLE 8

STRUCTURE OF THE ARTICLE 15

ARTICLE AND ITS TYPES 21

REQUIREMENTS FOR ACCEPTANCE OF SCIENTIFIC ARTICLES AND ABSTRACTS 24

RULES FOR PUBLISHING ARTICLES IN PRESTIGIOUS MAGAZINES 30

RECOMMENDATIONS ON WRITING THE TEXT IN A SCIENTIFIC STYLE 36

FINDING THE SCIENTIFIC PROBLEM AND CHOOSING THE TOPIC 42

LITERATURE STUDY AND REFERENCE LIST PROCEDURE 49

QUOTE 58

USEFUL SITES FOR RESEARCHERS 62

TASKS ON KNOWLEDGE GIVEN ON ARTICLE WRITING 65

CONCLUSION 71

REFERENCES 73

INTRODUCTION

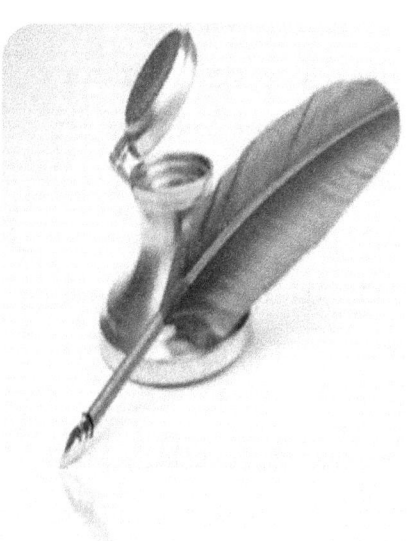

It is clear from history that every society or state tries to develop. If we look at development from the point of view of a small family, each family strives to live a healthy life, and each family member strives to find his place in society. If we look at the development from the point of view of the states, it strives to develop and build a society for its citizens that meets world standards. A developed society is realized with the help of science and technology discoveries invented by the mature representatives and scientists of that society, or at least in the current globalization process.

We know that the potential of information and communication technologies opens fundamentally new forms and possibilities of interaction and information exchange, helps to build and strengthen civil society, and accelerates the processes of economic reforms and democratic development of the country.

The Republic of Uzbekistan is striving to occupy a worthy place in the emerging global information society. In order to achieve these goals, the country's government has set strategic priorities for the activation of information processes in Uzbekistan, the rapid development of modern information and communication technologies, their introduction and use in all areas of the economy and society.

The development of the field of science was considered the most important task of all times. It is not difficult to understand that in a society where science does not develop, that society is heading towards extinction.

Scientific articles created by scientists play an integral role in the development of science. With the help of scientific articles, the foundation of any discovery is laid. Theoretical aspects are developed and applied in practice with the help of experiments.

A scientific article is an independent scientific research that expresses one's thoughts on a current scientific problem. The role of a scientific article is very important for people who have a high goal. That is, when we enter the university, we will get acquainted with a new environment, in short, we will fall into a new world, and we will be able to expand our goals by getting acquainted with a lot of achievements that can be achieved. For example, during the university period, for the first time, we get information about becoming state scholarship holders and we try to achieve it. One goal joins us and continues this way.

In scientific articles, the researcher's personal contribution to the development of the theoretical or practical foundations of modern science is expressed as clearly as possible.

The total number of published scientific works on the dissertation prepared for obtaining the degree of Doctor of Science (DSc) should not be less than 15, and at least 10 of them should be published in scientific publications, 1 of which should be a prestigious specialist of a foreign country with a developed branch of science should be published in scientific journals.

Nowadays, the interest of many people in our country to read articles and to write articles on any topic is certainly a gratifying thing.

GENERAL INFORMATION ABOUT THE ARTICLE

The article (from Arabic) is a journalistic genre. In the article, the events of social life are analyzed in depth, summarized theoretically and publicly, achievements in state policy, economy, technology, science and culture, advanced work experiences are publicized, and defects in the national economy are criticized. The main article, theoretical and propaganda article, problem article are widely used in the press. The Main Article (or the Article written by the editors) is the most responsible Article of the editorial office, which is tasked with conveying important issues of domestic and international life to the readership. This article is a guide on a specific issue

It should show, reveal the existing shortcomings, define the

main real way of each case. The article, the decrees of the President, the laws of the Oliy Majlis, the state and government documents, decisions, and laws adopted by the Cabinet of Ministers, the current issues of the time will be revealed in the main article. Theoretical Article and Propaganda The main task of the article is to describe the foundations and principles of the ideology of independence, the national idea, independence; The purpose of the scientific article is to explain and popularize the achievements of science, culture, and technology, and to raise the student's intellectual and scientific level. The problematic article is in the context of a discussion and debate, in which the author expresses his views on an issue.

An article is a genre of journalism, in which the author sets the task of analyzing social situations, processes, events, first of all, from the point of view of the underlying laws. In the article, the author considers individual situations as part of a wider phenomenon. The author discusses his point of view.

The article expresses the author's or editors' detailed, detailed, well-founded understanding of a current sociological problem. Also, in the article, the journalist should interpret the facts (these may be figures, additional information that puts the emphasis correctly and clearly reveals the essence of the matter).

The peculiarity of the article is its readiness. If the prepared material has never been published (not circulated, not distributed), then it is wrong to attribute such work to the article. Perhaps this work can be called a draft or a blank. Therefore, the purpose of any article is to spread the information contained in it.

There are five types of articles in modern journalism:

Editorial

The editorial represents the editorial point of view on the most pressing issue at the moment. The leading article helps to correctly address the problems of social life, answers the most urgent problems.

The main requirements: relevance of the topic, in-depth disclosure and justification of the proposed tasks, accuracy and conciseness of generalizations, conclusions, arguments.

Editors can be:

- general political – published in connection with important dates, events;
- promotion – revealing creative perspectives, implementing certain ideas;
- operational – reflects the most urgent political and economic tasks at the moment.

Research paper

A scientific and theoretical explanation of current events is given in examples of specific situations. Such articles analyze theoretical aspects of economy, politics, literature and art.

Informational article

Information-narrative – material, as a rule, is arranged in a sequence that corresponds to their temporal or spatial development, execution.

Information and description – published together with information and story or separately from it. In this type of article, information is presented in such a way that the reader has an idea about the subject of the description as a whole, as well as about its components, individual features and characteristics.

General Research Paper

This group includes publications analyzing broad issues of general importance. For example, the author of such an article can talk about the directions of political or economic development of the country, or about the level of morality that exists in society as a whole today, or about the possibility of the union of church and state. Or about the country's relations with foreign countries, etc. Publications of this type are characterized by a high level of generalization and the level of global thinking of the authors. The purpose of the general research article is to study various laws, trends and perspectives of the development of modern society. A general research article is a difficult genre in the sense that it requires not only knowledge of a specific problem, but also a theoretical explanation of its existence.

Practical and analytical article

It is primarily focused on actual practical problems of industry and life, agriculture, entrepreneurship, culture, science, education, business, finance, etc. These articles analyze specific problems, events, actions, situations related to practical tasks, in a specific field is decided: field of activity, industry, etc. The author sets himself the goal of determining the causes of the situation that has arisen in a specific field of production, in a number of enterprises, in the social sphere, etc., and to evaluate these situations. To determine their development trends.

The history of the article genre in Uzbekistan is mainly related to the «Gazette of the Turkestan Region». Various spheres of socio-political life are expressed in it (Furqat, Ibrat, Hakimkhan, etc.). Later, Hamza, Abdulla Avloni, Abdulla Qadiri and others participated in the progressive

Uzbek national press with their articles.

Currently In mass media, all types of articles are given. The article is a publication covering current topics.

The term article is broadly applied to scientific works in newspapers, magazines, radio, television, and collections.

Articles consist of three components:

1. Introduction – the relevance of the chosen topic is determined.
2. The main part – the idea, problem or innovation planned by the author is stated.
3. Conclusion – the author's conclusions and recommendations are given on the topic.

Articles are written in a scientific or journalistic style, fully following the norms of the literary language. When writing an article, it is important to define the topic of the article and choose a title for it. The title of the article should be short, but it should attract attention and, of course, highlight the main topic of the article. The article also provides a brief description of the author and a list of references.

STRUCTURE OF THE ARTICLE

Only scientific publications of the author are placed in journals. The authors take responsibility for the accuracy of the information provided in the articles, as well as the quality of the translation of the text into other languages. The editors of the journal are not responsible for any inaccuracies in the published works.

5 simple rules of article formatting:

Font size (Times New Roman) – size: 14.

Line spacing: 1.5.

All fields: 2.5.

Paragraph: 1.25.

The structure of the article includes the following points:

Article title.

Initials of the surname.

Full name in Russian / Full name in English, degree, title, position, department, place of work (study), city.

Keywords: key concepts covered in the article.

The text of the article.

List of references.

Summary of the content of the text (resumé)

Resume comes from the French word «résumé» and simply means a brief statement. A resume provides information about the person you are applying for, such as their name, education level, work experience, qualifications, etc.

A resume is the most important document in the search for a job. In Uzbek, such a document can also be called a «resumé» and a «personal reference», but the form of a resume is slightly different from these documents. A resume is primarily a document sent by job seekers when applying for a job, but it can be used for other purposes as well. For example, the resume of the director of the organization or the project manager is submitted to the donor organization together with the grant proposal.

The main parts of the resume are:
1. Personal information
    a. Name (required)
    b. Contact addresses: phone, email, place of residence (required)
    c. Gender (optional
    d. Nationality (optional)
    e. Date of birth (optional)

2. Summary and/or professional objective (optional)

    a. Summarize the most important points in a

sentence or two.

Structure of the article

I. Introduction

Of the subject Based on +

Of the subject relevance +

Main thesis

- Retrospective analysis of the given topic.

• Justification of the need to consider the topic from today's positions.

• Interpretation of the main concepts of the subject.

A statement of errors related to the statement of the subject, etc

II. The main part

Evidence+

put forward which confirms the thesis the facts • use of induction: from specific to generalization;

• use deduction: from general to detailed consideration.

III. The final part

Previously published which confirms the thesis or negative conclusions
• statement of the main idea in the form of theses;
• conclusions;
• show the duration of the problem

We will try to summarize the above ideas.

I. Introduction (10-20%)
• justification of the topic + relevance of the topic + main thesis
• retrospective analysis of the given topic.
• justification of the need to consider the topic from today's positions.
• explanation of the main concepts of the subject.
• statement of errors related to the description of the topic, etc

II. The main part (70-80 %)
• evidence + facts that support the proposed thesis
• use of induction: from specific to generalization;
• use deduction: from general to detailed consideration.

III. Final part (10-20 %)

• conclusions that confirm or deny the proposed thesis

• statement of the main idea in the form of theses;
• conclusions;
• show the duration of the problem;
• recommendations.

ARTICLE AND ITS TYPES

The article has a literary or scientific content and is quite large in terms of volume. The article can be devoted to important and topical issues of life or illuminate a field of science. Accordingly, the articles are divided into scientific, methodical, journalistic and scientific-popular types. Articles consist of three components:

1. Introduction – the relevance of the chosen topic is determined.
2. Basis- the second part is the idea, problem or innovation planned by the author.
3. Conclusion – the author's conclusions and recommendations are given on the subject.

The articles are written in a scientific or journalistic style, fully following the standards of the literary language. When writing an article, it is important to define the topic of the article and choose a title for it.

The title of the article should be short, but it should attract attention and, of course, highlight the main topic of the article. In addition, the articles contain brief information about the author and a list of references.

Scientific and scientific-popular articles provide clear, grounded, consistent information about all things and events in nature and social life. In it, it is important to describe the nature of the event, analyze it, determine the cause, prove it with evidence, and state the reasonable results.

Scientific and scientific-popular articles are mainly a genre specific to the scientific method. Special terms make up the lexicon of this style, in which passive verbs and sentences with complex constructions are widely used, with strict adherence to the literary norm.

The scientific method varies according to different fields of knowledge, as well as to whom it is intended. For example, fields of science are distinguished by certain conventional signs, formulas, and descriptive material. Books in a scientific style can be aimed only at specialists by providing information about science, or such scientific information can be aimed at the general public. A style that is understandable to the general public and has emotionality and imagery in the description of the image is considered a popular scientific style. Lectures, brochures and textbooks intended for the masses are manifestations of this style.

Special terms are rarely used in popular scientific articles (and when they are used, they are explained), ideas are explained in an interesting language, and artistic representation methods that provide imagery are used in the narrative.

REQUIREMENTS FOR ACCEPTANCE OF SCIENTIFIC ARTICLES AND ABSTRACTS

A scientific article is an independent scientific description of research, in which the author expresses his opinion on a current scientific problem, draws conclusions and provides evidence with pictures, graphs, figures.

Requirements for accepting scientific articles and theses:

1) The content of a scientific article must include the following:

1.1. Relevance of the research, existing problems within the topic.

1.2. Ways to solve the problem.

1.3. Science-based suggestions and recommendations.

1.4. Expected economic and social impact.

2) Scientific articles and theses must be carefully edited and comply with all technical requirements of formalization, including: - text editor – written in MS Word format;

- page – in A4 size, in the form of a book, leaving 20 mm from all sides;
 - font – Times New Roman, size (kegel) – 14
  - line spacing and spacing at the beginning of the letter – 1.5;
  - the abstract (Abstract) should be around 250-300 words and keywords should not exceed 5-8 phrases and should be in three languages (Uzbek, English, Russian)
  - the size of the scientific article and thesis should

not exceed a minimum of 5 pages and a maximum of 8 pages, pages should not be numbered;

- the scientific article should cover current topics related to the directions of the conference, which have not been published before;

- write the author's full surname, first and last name, academic degree and title, position, name of the scientific institution and organization in the upper right corner, and the name of the scientific article in the middle (in bold letters);

- the number of authors does not exceed three;

- the text of the article should contain an introduction, scientific research and methods, research results and its discussion, conclusion and a list of literature;

- all tables, charts and pictures are written in MS Word format, in Times New Roman font, their names are written below the charts and pictures, and the names of the tables are written above; - all graphs and charts should be in MS Excel format;

- references to sources in tables, pictures and graphics and references to them in the text;

- preparation of the list of used literature (References) in the APA system;

- links should be placed at the bottom of each page. Scientific articles and theses can be submitted in Uzbek, Russian or English.

More than two articles from one author (co-author) will not be accepted.

3) Submitted scientific articles and theses will be examined for compliance with the above requirements and will also be checked based on the anti-plagiarism program.

According to experts' conclusions, the materials deemed inappropriate will not be published and will not be returned to the author. Scientific articles and theses that are considered positive will be included in an electronic collection for publication and posted on official websites. To the authors of the positive article and the conference online directly a certificate will be sent to the e-mail addresses of those who participated in a lecture or presentation.

The author is personally responsible for the accuracy of the information provided in the text of the article.

Before you start writing, you need to understand how to write a research paper and what it is. A scientific article is a small study on a specific subtopic. There are three research papers:

- Empirical (real experience) is an article based on one's own experience.
- Scientific-theoretical – these are articles that describe the specific results of research.
- Reviews are articles that narrowly analyze advances in a specific field.

The main stages of working on the article

1 • Determination of the topic, its analysis, planning.

2 • Work on the first version of the article based on the plan
3 • End of work, text analysis, improvement, correction

Before writing an article, answer the following questions

- What conclusions should be drawn from the material?
- What will be the content of the work?
  - Why is the article written?

Article structure:

- Abstract
- Login
- Main part
- Summary
- Bibliography, Appendix

RULES FOR PUBLISHING ARTICLES IN PRESTIGIOUS MAGAZINES

Conditions and procedure for accepting articles.

The editorial office accepts scientific and popular materials in Uzbek and Russian languages for publication. When scientific articles, independent expertise and editing show a positive result, they will be included in the next issue of the magazine. In order to improve the quality of the magazine, all articles received by the editors are checked for plagiarism.

The journal publishes articles of high scientific

innovation, theoretical and practical importance. The main scientific results of the research should be described in the article. Their authors can be research scientists, doctoral students, graduate students, researchers.

The following materials are provided by the authors to the editors of the journal:

- the author's application to the editor-in-chief;

- printed interpretation of the article prepared according to the requirements;

- a set of computer files with photos, graphs, tables and other research information. The materials received by the editors are registered and within two weeks, a confirmation of receipt of the article is sent to the author (authors).

Requirements for preparation of articles
The main elements of the article:

- Title of the article: in Uzbek and/or Russian, reflecting the content of the article, centered, in capital letters.
- FIO/pseudonyms of the authors in Uzbek and Russian.

- Full name of the organization, city, country, email address.
- Abstract (in Uzbek and/or Russian) – 150-250 words (ordered by page width). It should include the relevance of the research topic, setting of the problem, research goals, research methods, results and main conclusions.

The text of the article is in Uzbek or Russian.

List of sources used.

Key words (up to 15 words and phrases, which should reflect the nature of the topic).

Abbreviations are not allowed, there should be no transliteration (nominal nouns are an exception), this also applies to annotations and key words.

Article structure. The article should be written in IMRAD (Introduction, Methods, Results and Discussion) format:

- Introduction (Introduction) – includes relevance of the research topic, literature review on the research topic, setting of the research problem, expression of research goals and tasks;
- Styles (Materials and Methods) – describes the methods and

drawings of observations that allow to show the results using the text of the article. Describes the materials and other conditions of observation (this is a description of the research methodology and justification of its choice);
- Results (Results) – presents the practical results (tests, graphs, diagrams, equations, photos, pictures) obtained during the conducted studies;
– Discussion (Discussion)
- consists of interpretation of research results, their analysis and comments on them;
- Conclusion (Conclusion) – has a short summary of the sections of the article, without repeating the expressions presented in them.

The volume of the text of the article consists of 10-15 pages in A4 format, including pictures, tables and graphics.

The text is prepared in the Word editor for Windows in .rtf or .doc format;
The number of pictures is 4 at most. The inscriptions under the picture are written in Russian and English in 12 kegels.
Images are provided in separate .jpeg format. The text of the tables is typed in Russian and English. If the pictures and tables do not belong to the author of course, a link should be

provided.

Information about the authors is provided in Russian and English: full FIO, academic degree, title, position, field of scientific and other interests, number of scientific articles, contact information, recommended books for reading

Margins: top and bottom – 2 cm;
Left – 3 cm; right – 1 cm.

The text of the article is available on paper and electronic media (disk, flash drive, e-mail).

File Requirements:

- The first author's last name in Russian is used as the file name (for example: Usmanova.doc).
- The names of the illustration files must correspond to their numbers in the text (for example: Fig. 1.jpeg).

- The editors accept the electronic interpretation of articles and photos in any medium.

The fact that an article is returned to the author for completion does not mean that it has been accepted for publication. After receiving the revised text, the manuscript will be reviewed again by the editorial board. The revised text is returned by the author to the editors with the original interpretation of the article, as well as answers to all comments. The day when the last version of the article is received by the editors is considered the date of receipt of the article.

The editor-in-chief has the right to select articles for publication.

RECOMMENDATIONS ON WRITING A TEXT IN A SCIENTIFIC STYLE

Preparation stage

At this stage, it is necessary to do the following:
- collecting information (reading, observing, talking, conducting a survey, etc.).
- Ideas about the issue that you can say about this topic

Collection and analysis;
- puzzle over how to write about it better (cluster, Construction of a conceptual scheme, etc.).

Stage 1

Creating a draft version of the work
At this stage, it is necessary to do the following:

• writing in drafts;
• pay attention only to your own ideas, do not get confused about the form and orthography, rules of expression for the time being
• writing with a line break: there is space for writing new text during editing.

Stage 2

Correction

This is the stage for improving the draft version. It consists of making notes and corrections to the draft. In this case, you will need to use indicators, clip additional sheets, and other methods to mark the areas of the draft that need to be corrected.

When editing, you should ask yourself the following questions:

- Does the entire content of the text relate to the main topic?
- Are there any areas where additional information is required?
- Shouldn't some words be added/left out to emphasize the main idea?
- Are ideas not clearly or superficially expressed?
- Is the text logically structured?
- Is the introduction clearly written?
- Is the conclusion believable, does it match the substance?
- Is the final part connected to the beginning of the text?

Stage 3

Editing or proofreading

This final stage begins after the drafting and proofreading of the text. Your task is to ensure that there are no spelling, grammatical and stylistic errors in the text. To do this, you should ask yourself the following questions:

- Are all the words spelled correctly? (Underline the words you are not sure how to spell and look them up in a dictionary.)

- Do all the sentences express a complete thought?
- Are there any long sentences, should they not be divided into separate sentences?
- Punctuation marks: commas, hyphens, colons, semicolons are placed correctly?
- Are all paragraphs indented? (Any new idea should start with a paragraph).

The main stages of working on the article:

1. Ability to choose the right topic;

- determination of the topic, its analysis, structure of the plan/theses.
- study the literature on the topic;
- collecting factual materials on the topic;

2. Work on the first version of the article based on the plan/theses

3. Completion of work, text analysis, improvement, correction.

Before you start writing your article, answer the following questions:

- what conclusion should be drawn from the material?
- what will be the content of the work?
- why is the article written?

«THE TITLE IS HALF THE SUCCESS»

The shorter the title, the better. Because the shorter, clearer and more meaningful the title is, the more readable and mature the scientific research is. On the contrary, a long and long title is one of the signs of inconvenient and sloppy work. The title should not contain redundant words.

Scientific conclusion is the essence, purpose and most necessary part of scientific research. A scientific conclusion is a scientific understanding formed by the researcher about the phenomenon observed and described by the researcher. The scientific conclusion must be concise, understandable, clear, based on the descriptions given by the researcher, and should be formed as a meaningful law.

Articles must be written in scientific style only by a third party.

In order for the scientific article to be of high quality and attract attention: - The topic of the article should be short, meaningful and attention-grabbing. – If the subject of the article includes commas (,), colons (and question marks (?), exclamation marks (!) punctuation marks, it attracts many people's attention and is highly appreciated. – Journals are mainly the authors' own

Note that they provide links to previously published articles in their journals. The reason is that a simple journal quickly gains status. That is, do a literature review using previously published articles in the journals you want to publish! It is interesting for both you and the magazine. – Avoid plagiarism.

FINDING THE SCIENTIFIC PROBLEM AND CHOOSING THE TOPIC

In the process of scientific research, certain difficulties are eliminated in the process of studying new phenomena, explaining previously unknown facts. Difficulties in scientific research are most clearly manifested in problematic situations where the level of existing scientific knowledge is insufficient to solve new knowledge problems.

The scientific problem is often and rightly described as «conscious ignorance». In fact, there is no problem as long as we are not aware of our own ignorance about a phenomenon. They appear with the understanding that there are gaps in our knowledge that can be filled by further development of science and successful efforts in practice.

So, a scientific problem is a form of scientific knowledge, the content of which is not yet known to man, but it is necessary to know. A scientific problem is a difficulty that can only be solved by research. The narrow meaning of this concept: «scientific problem» is a form of thinking that describes the inadequacy of existing means to achieve the goal of scientific knowledge.

The problem is not a frozen form of knowledge, but a process that includes two main points – its formation and solution. Finding, formulating and solving problems are the main features of scientific activity.

In science, no problem is created from scratch; This is determined by the prior knowledge and prevailing values of the researchers. Scientific formulation of the problem requires previously collected empirical materials, developed theories and methods.

The following conditions are necessary for the correct formulation and formulation of the problem:

- the presence of previous scientific knowledge that can be included in the studied problem;
- its formally correct construction, that is, expression of the main meaning of the problem;
- correctness of the problem, that is, its premises should not be false; not a global problem, but a sufficient limitation;
- conditions of the solution (methods, methods, means) and indicators of its verification methods

The topic is a short and clear statement of the nature of the problem (or part of it) to be solved in the research.

It is generally accepted that choosing the right topic is half the guarantee of its successful implementation. The topic should be relevant, distinguished by novelty, direct scientific research into the field of vital, but unsolved problems and issues of modern science and practice. The relevance and compatibility of scientific and practical requirements is a serious criterion for choosing a research topic. From the point of view of the modern requirements of scientific and professional activity, the artificial subjects of scientific research, disconnected from life, do not justify themselves.

The subjective factor should also be taken into account when choosing a research topic. Personal interest, existing positive experience in the chosen thematic area is a powerful incentive that mobilizes the researcher's strength and guarantees the achievement of the desired results.

It is possible to formulate certain requirements for the selection and formation of the topic of scientific research:

1) Relevance (newness, relevance to community life,

consideration of social needs when solving an urgent conflict);

2) Specificity (the real existence of the studied object, the accuracy, precision, accuracy and correctness of its definition of its subject);

3) Problematic (the presence of a problematic side in the topic, consisting of the need to search for ways and mechanisms to resolve the conflict);
4) Clarity of concepts (unclear, polysemantic and vague definitions are not allowed)
5) Brevity (brevity of formulating the topic in harmony with content capacity).

A topic is a scientific issue that covers a specific area of problems that requires research. It is based on many research questions – rather small scientific questions related to a specific problem area. When solving a problem or issue, a specific research task is solved, for example, the development of a new material, construction, advanced technology, and so on. In this case, their implementation is not only of theoretical importance, but also of practical importance with a certain expected economic effect.

A number of requirements are imposed on the topic of scientific research:

It is necessary that the topic is relevant and needs to be solved at the moment. There are currently no relevant criteria for determining the level of relevance of topics related to fundamental research. Therefore, relevance in this case is determined by a major scientist or scientific community.

As for the practical description of the topic, their relevance is usually determined by the development and economic efficiency requirements of a specific branch of production.

The topic should solve a new scientific problem and have a description of scientific innovation.

Economic efficiency and relevance are important requirements for a scientific topic. Subjects related to applied research should have an estimated economic effect at the stage of selection. When choosing a topic of fundamental description, the criterion of economic efficiency gives way to the criterion of importance.

The topic should be relevant to the scientific direction. This allows to make the most complete use of the competence and authority of the scientific team. As a result, the theoretical level, quality and economic efficiency of the development will increase, and the duration of the research will be shortened.

Current maturity is an important description of the topic. The developers of the topic must determine the possibility of its completion in the planned period and determine its introduction into the customer's production environment. They should be familiar with the relevant production, its current and future requirements.

The selection of the topic is based on the sources of domestic and foreign literature, that is, on the issue being resolved. It is accompanied by careful study. This is necessary in order not to reinvent the bicycle, as well as to determine the direction of modern scientific research.

The objective factors that motivate the choice of the topic are as follows:

- demand for social development;
- demand for scientific and technical development;
- the need for a social and political system;
- factor of economic development;
- the need for cultural development.

LITERATURE STUDY AND REFERENCE LIST PROCEDURE

Work on literary sources is a part of research activity at all stages of scientific research, and it can be singled out as the first stage of any scientific research work. Studying literature allows to choose and clarify the problem, to determine the direction of study; study the history of the issue, get acquainted with different points of view, «identify white spots», define the problem area of the research, study the current state of the issue and the level of development of individual aspects, get acquainted with various methods. Pedagogical research, collection of factual and statistical materials.

Searching for the necessary literature occurs when studying or viewing the following publications and sources:

- theses or scientific lectures, collections of works;
— collective or individual monographs;
- professional magazines such as primary school, primary education (the last issue of the year contains a list of published materials);
- the list of literature used in graduation qualification or

dissertation work;

— websites of publishers and reference publications;

— reference-bibliographic sections of libraries (alphabetical, systematic, thematic catalogs);

— network resources, etc.

A literature review in a scientific work is necessary to show the experience of the author's predecessors and to identify shortcomings in the study of the chosen topic. In addition, the purpose of studying literature is to ensure that the author does not work in vain by repeating the research of other scientists, but has the opportunity to increase his scientific knowledge on the current problem and make his own contribution.

The list of references is compiled in alphabetical order by the last name of the author, first by national literature, then by foreign, and then by Internet sites. References to all sources in the bibliography [1] in the text of the abstract should be indicated, where 1 is the number of the source in the list.

No matter how narrow and specific the topic, the search for material for its development can continue indefinitely. To narrow the scope of the search, you need to analyze the information and choose the most necessary.

It is advisable to get acquainted with the literature in the following sequence: guiding documents (first laws, then legal documents), scientific publications (first books, then periodicals), statistical data. You should familiarize yourself with the sources in reverse chronological order, that is, it is recommended to study the most recent publications first, then last year, then two years ago, and so on.

A bibliographic description is a set of information about the source, given in accordance with certain rules defined by the standard, and necessary for describing the document and searching for it. Elements of bibliographic description combined in regions are separated by a colon. In each field, the description elements are given in a certain sequence and are separated from each other by appropriate delimiters.

It is recommended to provide a list of references to the work as a whole. The list must be numbered. Each, regardless of how often it appears in the text of the work the source is mentioned once in the list.

The most convenient arrangement of the material is in alphabetical order, because in this case the works are collected in author collections. The works of the same author are listed alphabetically by title.

Official documents are placed at the beginning of the list in a certain order: Constitution; Codes; Laws; Presidential decrees; Government decision; other regulatory documents (letters, orders, etc.). Within each group, documents are arranged in chronological order.

Literature in foreign languages is placed at the end of the list after literature in Russian, forming an additional alphabetical line.

The following bibliographic description elements are provided for each document: author's surname, initials; title; title data (textbook, study guide, dictionary, etc.); trace (place of publication, publisher, year of publication); quantitative characteristic (total number of pages in the book).

Official documents.
Constitutions, conventions, treaties, agreements, concepts, doctrines:
Universal Declaration of Human Rights. – Moscow: Human Rights, 1996. – 16 p.
Legal documents: On librarianship: Federal Law of December 29 No. 78-FZ. 1994: Adopted by the State Duma

on November 23. 1994 // Collection of legal documents of the Russian Federation. – 1995. – No. 1. – Art. 2. One city and two publishers

Vakulenko L.S. Education and training of children with speech disorders. Psychology of children with speech disorders: studies. Method. Pension / L. S. Vakulenko. – Moscow: FORUM: INFRA-M, 2019. – 271 p.

No publisher information available

Simonenko V.E. Connection schemes in Russian folk choirs and round dances: a graphic guide / V.E. Simonenko. – St. Petersburg: [p. And.], 1998. – 11 p. : ill.

Books with two authors:

Kay S. Inside Out: Student's book: Upper intermediate / S. Kay, W. Jones. – Oxford: Macmillan Heinemann, 2001. – 160 p.

Collections:

Peace and War: Essays in Russian History. Owls.

Dramaturgy 1946-1980 / RAS, State. Institute of Art History; answer ed. I. L. Vishnevskaya. – Moscow: Lenand, 2009. – 287 p.

Dissertations and theses:

Eliner I. G. The development of multimedia culture in the information society: the author. Dis. ... Doctor of cultural sciences: 24.00.01 / Eliner Ilya Grigorievich; SPbGUKI. – St. Petersburg, 2010. – 34 p.

Notes:

Tchaikovsky P. I. Maid of Orleans: an opera in 4 days (6 cards) / P. I. Tchaikovsky; ed. Text: F. Schiller, V. A. Zhukovsky. – Piano. – Moscow: Ed. P. Jurgenson, 1880. – 205 p. : notes.

Maps and atlases:

Atlas on the history of the Middle Ages: (with a set of contour maps) / comp. And prepare. To the editor. «Kartography» PKO in 1970; answer ed. E. N. Regentova. – That's right. In 1999 – M.: Roskartografiya, 2000. – 1 atl. (20 p.)

Dictionaries and encyclopedias:

New Russian encyclopedia. T. 8 (2) in 12 volumes. Unity – Costa Ricans / ed. A. D. Nekipelov. – Moscow: Encyclopedia, 2011. – 480 p. : ill.

The list of used literature is a collection of bibliographic information about the documents (book, thesis, article) cited according to the established rules, which are necessary for the individual identification and general characterization of the document.

The order of the bibliography consists of fixed and immutable headings and elements. The document contains fields in the following order:

The title of the statement, in which the author(s) name(s) or collective name is given;

Information on title and responsibility; title and related information; information about the persons and organizations involved in the creation of the document;

The field of information about the function of the

publication, reprint, its characteristics;

Area of information about the place of publication, publisher, year of publication;

Number characteristics area, which includes information about the document size and illustrative material;

. – (dot and dash) – comes before all areas except the first one;

: - (colon) – the information related to the title is placed before the name of the publisher;

/ - (slash) – is placed before the information about responsibility. (authors, compilers, editors, translators, organizations involved in the publication).

// - (two slashes) – information about the document in which the main part is located is placed before it. (article, chapter, section).

The elements of the bibliography list contain punctuation that conforms to language norms.

To make references fields and items clearer, a space character is used before and after the conditional character. There are three types of bibliography:

Under the name of the individual author;
Under the name of the collective author;
Under the title.

QUOTE

Quotation is the inclusion of someone else's written or spoken speech in the author's text. The editor's work with quotations is the reading of someone else's speech in the text has properties related to the evaluation of the original and the verification of the accuracy of its repetition. This allows us to classify it as a special type of factual material.

By tradition, editing is considered a direct quotation, i.e. repeating someone's speech verbatim. In the written text, it is necessarily enclosed in quotation marks that indicate its beginning and end, in the spoken text it is preceded by and ends with replicas. No less than a direct quote, an indirect quote is a repetition, i.e. conveying the main meaning of someone else's speech in your own words. The requirements for the correctness of the meaning of direct and indirect quotations are the same. An allusive quotation can refer to an indirect quotation – a well-known text rewritten where the original source is easily seen.

The editor who begins working with quotations evaluates their place and purpose in the text, their connection with the author's speech, and the appropriateness of quoting.

According to their role in the text, rhetorical quotations can be conditionally divided. Their purpose is to create an image of the author of the quoted statements or to describe something or an event using quotes from respected, famous people. A classic example of such a quote is A.E. Milchin – K.I. literary portraits created by Chukovsky in his book «Contemporaries». In the oral portrait of A.P. There are almost more Chekhov quotes than the author's text, and this leads to a surprising phenomenon – the effect of the writer's presence. Such quoting requires extraordinary skill, because the author's speech, methods of quoting into the text must match the level of the quoted original. When the juicy, lively language of the quote is combined with the vague, vague language of the author, it primarily characterizes the latter, and not in any good way.

In mass media texts, there is often another combination – the speech of a malicious author creates a less successful statement of someone. A quote is used as a means of describing a famous person, as a rule, to discredit the latter. Often arbitrarily torn from the text. This is a powerful rhetorical device, so a hastily uttered and ill-conceived phrase turned out to be very quickly beaten in the headlines: «a squiggle at a price of 188 million»; «Zagogulin in bronze

– there is a vertical of power: in the monument project of the Yeltsin era». In this case, the editor faces the ethical and aesthetic problem of the sense of proportion.

In advertising and public relations texts, a quotation is used as a rhetorical device to create a positive attitude towards a product or service. It is known that the testimony of a respected person in favor of something is always more weighty and reliable than a simple text of the same content. Let's recall the TV commercial about the American scientist Linus Pauling, which was little known to the Russians at that time. But it's one thing to simply announce that a scientist is a two-time Nobel laureate, and it's completely different in terms of the effect the ad writers have on the audience. They cited Albert Einstein's statement about Pauling's personality and his contributions to science. In this way, the image of a bright scientist almost like Einstein was formed. And all this was needed to sell the vitamins and nutritional supplements created by Pauling.

A quotation is used not only as a rhetorical device, but also to convey information. The author refers to it as a justification for any rules of the text or as the main source of valuable facts.

In this case, the editor will decide whether the quote really confirms the judgments made or not, whether the conclusion from the quote is correct or not, whether the ideas of the text and the quote match or not, and the author has his own opinion on the topic. Should evaluate whether to replace his research with an unlimited article. References to authority, whether he is in a hurry to hide behind his predecessors, to enter the beaten path. In this case, indulging in nails is harmful.

The text looks like a collection of chaotic fragments of someone else's speech, behind which the individuality of the author is not visible, the integrity and coherence of the presentation is lost. If a quote is used as a source of facts, it will be evaluated like any other factual material.

Quotations that serve only to convey some information are often illustrative material and are not included in the conceptual part of the text. They should be appropriate, should fully correspond to the idea of the text, should not lead to unnecessary associations and should not overload the text. This applies not only to direct quotations enclosed in quotation marks, but also to indirect quotations. Evaluation of quotations compliance with all these requirements is the editor's first step in working with them.

USEFUL SITES FOR RESEARCHERS

www.scirus.com

Scirus is one of the most comprehensive science search engines on the Internet. Performs a full-text search through journal articles (over 380 million indexed pages) of most major foreign publishers.

Scholar.google.com

Search system of scientific literature. It includes articles from major scientific publishers, archives of print publications, publications on the websites of universities, scientific societies and other scientific organizations and calculates the citation index of publications.

www.scienceresearch.com/search

A scientific search engine that performs full-text searches of journals from many major scientific publishers, including Elsevier, Highwire, IEEE, Nature, Taylor & Francis, and more. Searches articles and documents in open scientific databases: Open Access Journal Catalog, Library of Congress

Online Catalog, Science.gov, and Science News.

www4.infotrieve.com

Search over 35,000 journal articles in physics, engineering, medicine, law, and more. You can only search for a specific field of science.

SciGuide: http://www.prometeus.nsc.ru/sciguide/

Electronic navigator of foreign scientific electronic resources of open access on the Internet. The structure of the navigator and its content were jointly developed by the employees of the Department of Foreign Literature Acquisition of the Siberian Department of the Russian Academy of Sciences and the Department of the State Public Scientific and Technical Library.

Grammarly.com

A program that checks an English scientific article and shows errors

Turnitin.com – helps to detect plagiarism (in foreign

languages)

Antiplag.uz is a national anti-plagiarism system

Quillbot.com is a platform for rewriting and expressing words

Wordtune.com is a site that enriches the ideas you want to write

TASKS ON THE KNOWLEDGE GIVEN ON ARTICLE WRITING

Task 1. According to the «Complex of Thoughts» technology, combine the ideas given below into separate topics depending on their content.

- Scientists say that after sunset on December 21, 2020, the planets Jupiter and Saturn will approach each other at a minimum distance in the night sky for the first time since the Middle Ages.

- According to information, the robotic dolphin weighs 270 kilograms, and its battery lasts for 10 hours. In salt sea water, the device can work for about 10 years. It not only reproduces the movements of real dolphins, but also does not differ from this mammal in its muscles and skeleton. All movements of the robot are controlled by the operator, and to ensure its autonomy in the future, it will be necessary to install a camera, sensors and an artificial intelligence system.

- Two gas giants come close to each other every 20 years. But they rarely approach each other at a minimum distance. The last time such convergence happened on March 4, 1226.

From December 16 to 25, the distance between Jupiter and Saturn will be about one-fifth of a full moon from Earth, and the two planets will appear as if they are a double planet.

- Many users on the Internet claim that the newly created robot-dolphin is over-realized and even suspect the authors of the project of forgery.

- Residents of the Equator will have the best conditions for observing this phenomenon, but it will be possible to observe it from any part of the world, weather permitting. The planets begin to appear in the western sky an hour after sunset. The further north the observer is located, the less time he has to observe this phenomenon before the planets move beyond the horizon.

- The robot was ordered by one of the country's aquariums due to the ban on the trade of wild animals as part of the fight against the pandemic in China. In general, the authors of the project predict that such robots will become popular even after the pandemic.

- Experts say that the next time the planets will come close to each other on March 15, 2080, and then again only in 2400 years.

Task 2. Cluster into article types.

Task 3. Rewrite the article by connecting the given parts of the text in terms of content.

Abu Rayhan Beruni (973-1048)

- Besides his mother tongue, Beruni learned several other languages: Arabic, Sugdian, Persian, Syriac, Greek and ancient Oriya languages, and later Sanskrit in India.

- He was forced to leave his homeland at the age of 22 and lived as an emigrant in the city of Jurjan on the southeastern coast of the Caspian Sea for some time. Then he went to the ancient city of Ray, and after 998 he came back to Jurjan, where he met his second teacher, the physician, astronomer, philosopher Abu Sahl Isa al-Mashiy, and received education from him. Beruni «Osor al-Baqiya an alqurun al-Khaliya» («Monuments left by ancient peoples») as he started writing the poem during his emigration in Jurjon and finished it in 1000. «Osor al-Baqiya» brought great fame to Beruni, showing him to be a great scientist interested in all fields of science. In addition, Beruniy wrote more than 10 works on the history of astronomy and netrology in Jurjon.

- The great encyclopedic scholar of the Middle Ages, Abu Rayhan Muhammad ibn Ahmed al-Biruni, deeply studied a number of sciences of his time: astronomy, physics, mathematics, geodesy, mineralogy, geology, history, etc. He was born in Kat, the ancient capital of Khorezm, and his interest in science grew from a young age. Beruni later studied under the famous scholar Abu Nasr Mansur ibn Iraq. Ibn Iraq wrote a number of works on astronomy, geometry, and mathematics, dedicating 12 of them to Beruni.

- Beruni took an active part in the country's political affairs as the closest advisor to Shah Mahmud Ghaznavi II.

- After compiling the list of his works, Beruni wrote two more important books. One of them is Mineralogy. For its meaning, this treatise is considered the best, unrivaled work in the field of mineralogy in Central Asia and the Middle East, and even in Europe. The manuscript of Beruni's last work, «The Book of Medicinal Plants», was found in Turkey in the 30s of the 20th century. The work is known as «Saydona», it gives a full description of the medicinal plants that grow in the Near East, especially in Central Asia.

- The capture of Khorezm by Mahmud Ghaznavi put Beruni's life in danger. He was taken to the city of Ghazna along with all the scholars of Khorezmshah's palace. Beruni's life in Ghazna in the years 1017-1048, on the one hand, was finally difficult, but on the other hand, it was the most productive period for his scientific activity. Beruni's work «Famous People of Khorezm» was also created during this period. His important astronomical-geographical work «Tahdid nihiyot al-amonia li tashidi disat al-masokin» («Determining the final limits of places to check the distance between settlements» - «Geodesy») was completed in 1025.

Task 4. Compose a text according to the method of «composing a text based on concepts».

Create microtexts independently using the key words and phrases given below on the topic «Great figures of Central Asia».

1) Khorezm, Baghdad Academy, observatory, decimal system, four operations, algorithm, algebra;
2) Samarkand, eight works, «Movement of heavenly bodies and the science of stars», manual of

astronomy;

3) Farob, Damascus, Egypt, more than 160 works
4) City of Kat, Ma'mun Academy, foreign languages, about 200 scientific works, globe, «Relics of ancient peoples», «India», Treasury;
5) Sayram, Yassi, 23 years old, «Proverbs».

CONCLUSION

Nowadays, the question arises among some people that why articles are needed. Below we will try to find an answer to this question.

Over the past half century, humans have made great strides in cybernetics, but today we are still getting closer to understanding how to make working code understandable and reusable, how to connect tons of different information, and how the brains of even the simplest organisms work. . Even the smallest breakthrough in these areas promises huge competitive advantages. Because of this, tech companies are growing by leaps and bounds. And not some specially trained scientists, but almost ordinary programmers work in them. The only difference is that they work at the beginning of development. There is no «pure» science here, and the line between scientists and engineers is obscenely blurred.

The main way to share information about progress is through scientific journals. So if you're doing great work and want the right people and the world to know about it, you need to publish it. The more results you share with the world, the higher your professional credibility and the more likely you are to be the best candidate to lead the creation of the first production batch of biorobots to take over the world tomorrow. It should not be thought that only graduate students, candidates of sciences and doctors can publish lots of great articles written by young and brave seniors. By the way, the availability of a good publication is one of the main criteria to evaluate if you want to do an internship on the other side of the Earth for six months before graduation or just plan to study.

However, scientific publishing is not easy. The fact is that when you sit down to write an article, you will not only create interesting ideas, but also demonstrate your ability to critically evaluate them and draw unbiased conclusions. Most people don't know how to do it. It's not enough to write an article – you need to be able to present it in a way that experts want to read. Therefore, if you are sure with the article you should go to a DIY conference, where you will be greeted by an intereseted crowd of these professionals. They ask awkward questions and you convince them you're right. Often it helps you look at what you're doing and how you're doing it in a very different way. And at conferences, you can make many important acquaintances that will be very useful in the future.

REFERENCES :

1. O'zbekiston milliy ensiklopediyasi. 2000-2005;
2. Signallarga spektrial ishlov berishning tezkor algoritmlarining dasturiy kompleksini yaratish. Samarqand – 2014;
3. Axborot va axborotlashtirishga oid normativ-huquqiy hujjatlar to'plami. //To'plovchilar: A.I.O'ralov, M.I.Ishbekov, D.S.Sa'dullayev. –Toshkent, "Adolat" nashriyoti, 2008.
4. Л.А.Залманзон. Преобразования Фурье, Уолша, Хаара и их применение в управлении, связи и других областях.М «Наука» Главная редакция Физико- Математической литературы.1989
5. Акоста В., Кован К., Грэм Б. Основы современной физики. М.: Просвещение, 1981.495с.
6. www.uz.m.wikipedia.org
7. www.hozirgi.org
8. www.fayllar.org
9. https://delovyelyudi.ru/uz/chasy/chto-takoe-antiplagiat-rabotaem-s-izobrazheniem/
10. http://spcenter.uz/uz/page/184URL
11. https://fayllar.org/toshkent-axborot-texnologiyalari-universiteti-samarqand-filial-v3.html
12. https://apastyle.apa.org

www.ingramcontent.com/pod-product-compliance
Lightning Source LLC
LaVergne TN
LVHW010606070526
838199LV00063BA/5096